My First Chicken Book

JENNY KELLETT

Scan above to check out our other books!

My name is...

Hey there!
I'm Cami
the chicken.

Welcome to the farm! I'm excited to show you around my world and share some egg-citing facts about chickens!

Chickens live on <u>farms</u> and in <u>backyards</u> all around the world.
Have you ever seen a chicken?

How many chickens can you see on the farm? Count them! 1, 2, 3....

Chickens are birds. They have feathers and wings, but they're not great flyers!

There are lots of different types of birds!

Can you <u>match</u> these birds to their shadows?

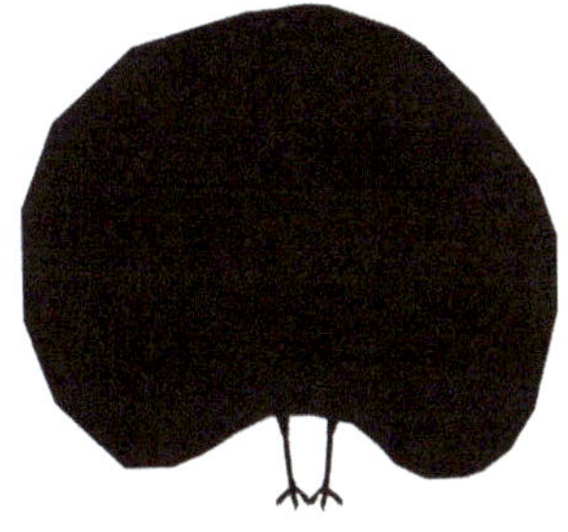

Chickens can be many **different colors**, such as black, **white** and **brown**. Some even have extra fluffy feathers to keep warm!

Odd One Out
Which of these is
not a chicken?
Can you name the odd one out?

I lay eggs and say *cluck cluck*!
Female chickens are called hens.

Male chickens are called roosters.

Which is which?! Point to the hen and the rooster!

Can you
cock-a-doodle-doo
like a rooster?!

Chickens eat grass, seeds, and sometimes even small bugs!

What's **your** favorite food? Is it the same as the chicken's?

Can you *draw a line* from the chicken to its favorite foods?

Chickens are very social animals and love spending time with their flock.

What do chickens love to do?

Scratching in the dirt

Sharing a meal

Exploring

Being with friends

Baby chickens are called chicks.
Chicks hatch from eggs!

These animals also have chicks!

Can you match the
baby chicks to their parents?

Penguin

Flamingo

Duck

A **chicken coop** is a safe and cozy home for chickens! It keeps them warm and protects them from danger.

One chicken in this coop is different!
Can you find it?

Did you know chickens can lay eggs in many colors? Some eggs are **white**, some are **brown**, and some are even **blue** or **green**!

Can you color in this hen and her eggs in lots of different colors?!

Scrambled Eggs
Omelet
Eggs are yummy and good for you!
How do you like to eat your eggs?
Fried Egg
Boiled Egg

Can you count all the eggs hiding in this picture?

Cami is tired!

Can you help her find her cozy coop?

Trace the path with your finger that leads Cami to her coop.

Lookout for the scarecrow!

Fun Facts About Chickens

Mother hens cluck to their chicks before they hatch, and the chicks chirp back!

Chickens can run really fast!

Chickens love rolling around in dirt to keep their feathers clean.

CONNECT THE SAME PICTURE

What's your favorite thing about chickens?

Can you name two foods that chickens eat?

Do you remember what baby chickens are called?

Congratulations!
Name: ....
For learning all about
CHICKENS
And becoming a Certified Chicken Expert
Jenny Kellett
Author

ALSO BY JENNY KELLETT

... and more!

Scan here to discover more books!

Available at

www.bellanovabooks.com

and all major online bookstores.

We'd love to hear from you!

If you and your child enjoyed this book, we'd love to hear from you!

Leaving a **quick review** takes just a few seconds and makes a world of difference for us.

As an independent author, your support helps us create more fun and educational books. **Thank you!**

Leave a Review

Scan me